Sakura

# Sakura

Myriam San Marco

Burning Eye

Credits

'Prologue' was originally published as 'Murder' in *The Interpreter's House* 58, February 2015.

'Never Gentle' was originally published in *The Interpreter's House 62*, June 2016.

'The Girl' was commissioned by the BBC for National Poetry Day 2016, under the title 'Marie-Rose'.

'Five Things' was originally published, with slight alterations, in *The Poet's Republic 3*, summer 2016.

'Image Is Everything' was originally published in *Boscombe Revolution* 3, Hesterglock Press, January 2015.

'Crossed Road', 'Snafu', 'If You Tell' and 'Forty-Eight' were originally published in *I am not a silent poet*, June 2015.

'Like a Ton of Lego Bricks' was originally published in *Message in a Bottle*, April 2015.

'You Hide, You Count' was originally published as 'You Hide, I Count' in *Oddity* 10, March 2015.

# CONTENTS

# PROLOGUE

Last night, limping, I walked. All the way to the edge
of myself, scheming how to get out of this hellish
crab bucket, these last ten years corroding the alloy slag
of an ordinary day. It felt cold. My gun stashed into
the back of the wheelhouse. Hands shaking, I saw the tears
stammering behind your eyes when I winched the rope out.
From that moment, there was no going back. The fear,
like a crouching adder, coiled around your lips,
inviting you to kneel. *Hands behind your back*, I said,
forcing a black hood over your head. It was tender,
the two shots to the back of the neck, one to the heart.
Twisting my ankle, shoving you off the ship, I felt
a kiss on my cheek, you floating away. Free, I cried.

A kiss on your cheek, me floating away free. You cried
twisting your ankle, shoving me off the ship. I felt
the two shots to the back of the neck, one to the heart,
forcing a black hood over my head. It was tender,
inviting me to kneel, hands behind my back. You said,
like a crouching adder coiled around my lips,
*From this moment, there is no going back*. The fear
stammering behind my eyes. When you winched the rope out
the back of the wheelhouse, hands shaking, I saw the tears
of an ordinary day. It felt cold, your gun. Stashed into the
crab bucket, these last ten years, corroding the alloy slag
of yourself, scheming. How to get out of this hellish
last night? Limping, you walked all the way to the edge.

SAKura
en (2017)
Hiver (2018)
TEMPÉTUEUX
effet
d'Ana, Bruno, Carmen, David, Eleanor et des
autres... A18

# SAKURA

I'll start up slow.
My thoughts under cover of snow grasping
at consciousness and vocal cords I don't possess.
I stand here. Rooted.
Stretching my bud-finger growth to catch sunlight.
My low branches turn to the skies.
My roots dig deep.
My sap will rise.
It's winter still. I stand here at the edge of the wood,
let foxes make their home in the hollow
of my back, invite migrating sparrows to nest
in my shoulders, and in the hole by my ankles
hedgehogs sleep.

Near sunset, the boy crunches the hill to speak to me
once more. He walks as if bees had told him their secret
dance, all jaggedy footsteps and eyes bent out of shape.
He rubs his hands on my bark, face pressed in knots and grooves,
resting forehead to lips across the grain. He flings sentence
after sentence at me in dew-spattered words, biting like African
red ants, hands to fists, knuckles scraping.

I can't talk back and his story hangs in the air between us.

Sakura is my name. I am the tree who listens.

*Let me tell you a story.*

*Once upon a time, a boy met a girl and fell in love with her.*

*Most stories start like this.*

*A face. Eyes touching eyes. A few shy smiles.*

*But there is the way skin can smell after bodies spent all day running in my forest and the way ozone presses down on blades of grass before a storm and the way the wind can crack even stones.*

*And there is the iron tang of blood.*

*I am the tree who listened.*

# HOW TO FALL IN LOVE - PART 1

Observe night and summer.

Drink bubbles and whistle.

Strain for the blackest-coldest-head-first throat of a hangover.

Look and ooze in envy.

Fall and lean. Lean and fall.

Inspect hands, eyes, lips, teeth and tongue.

Dawdle in the taproom.

It's morning; stroll on request.

Sip and linger.

Wake.

# HOW TO FALL IN LOVE – PART 2

Firstly strip off the layers of protection:
daydreaming, denials, rational thoughts and lust.

Peel the outer defence mechanisms off. Throw away.

Separate dreams one by one to slice through
the length of happy endings using Disney cutters.

Remove isolation and connect each nerve ending
marked in red to the correct emotion. Twist tightly.

Add liberal quantities of alcohol.

Watch for sparks. Repeat until the desired effect.

Make sure there are no loose connections.
It's often easier to add heat one screw turn at a time.

Some hearts will only have two settings. Some will have more.

Remember to slit the heart of a person lengthways
with a sharpened knife, being careful to not cut through.

# THE BOY

He had a stare that could catch waves and ride them.
He had eyes like funfair clamouring how he hated
to lose more than he liked to win. He looked me up and down
from the outside in, arms folded tight against his chest.

His mouth had a quirk when he lied, and he laughed
from a corner of his painted face. Tears all unsaid,
chin bold and bright giving the shimmy to his plastic life.
This boy had *don't see me* tattooed on his forehead
and skin taut with expectations waiting to be crushed.

He had such loud hands that they sang acapella
caressing the tumbleweed of his words. This boy.
He forgave the blisters on his palms after he nailed shut
all the doors and windows of his cardboard cut-out heart.
Before he could write his name in starlight, he'd buried

firm fingertips to loose elbows in the belly of the scrapheap.
He danced like a dragonfly fighting the mud throwers
from the bottom of his pond life with knees like brass bells,
legs like May bugs running as fast as a boomerang hoping
to take flight. He had a back alley flowing through the fabric

of his shoulders as red and as dark as lava. He had muscles
that would twitch, knuckles that could punch through concrete,
but he would flinch from open hands. He gnawed at my heart
like a dog who begs for scraps and cannot see the table is
buckling from the weight of the meat. This boy.

# THE GIRL

They called me Marie Rose.

I chased dreams like they were loaded culverins,
sailor boys with eyes like faucets and smiles of the deep blue.
I stretched my flying jibs to hug the sea and rolled down
waves to catch the light beyond the horizon.

Eyes closed, I felt for the flutter between kisses.

They said *fire* and *heave-ho* and *ready about* and *dead ahead.*
They said *bear away* and *loose the ballast* and *captain's on deck.*
They said *we need the black gang* and *ready the bimmies.*
They said *who is paying the devil?* and *abandon ship!*
They said many things that day as I sank in the Solent.

I struck a hint of blue and broke myself wishing.

They call me Marie Rose.
They say how beautiful
my guns and hail-shot pieces.
They say many things today.

# FIVE THINGS

I love that she smiles past the tears she keeps in,
dance-steps waiting to burst, raucous in her stride.
*But mostly, it's her lips.*

I love the way her soft hands rub my jagged angles
when she hugs – gentle – my deep-seated baggage.
*And the curve of her neck when it disappears under her shirt.*

I love to watch her scrutinise stars, dissecting the
inside of quarks that wrinkle the edge of her thoughts.
*It's the fire of her mind and the ways I don't burn.*

I love when she falls silent, the tender quiet in the
black of her eyes snowflaking the clang of my words.
*It's the pain in the words I don't say and the hurt in the ones she write*

I love how she sits – easy – in my kitchen, coffee in hand,
face all rumpled. Together we're writing our tomorrows.
*It's the way that we talk with our eyes.*

But mostly, it's her lips.

# IMAGE IS EVERYTHING

Hey, you!

You up there on the statue, can I take a few shots for *The Times*?
No, not with the girl. Just you.

Do you see me?

I see you ninja-stylee spiked red hair swagger – front-page priority.
CK boxers peeping out of black skinny jeans,
knees poking out of your eighteen holes – mean

I see you plastic gangster scowl tell no tales – headline ready.
I see studied bravado round your smuggler's smile,
stormy grey eyes sharpened to a point – fragile.

I see you wired ripples relentless bantam weight – newsworthy.
I see fear-tangled hands fiddling your missile-full kitbag.
Yeah, baby, I see you. I've Instagrammed your strut – right.

# COURTING BEDLAM

I wish I knew why the world around us is so preoccupied with celebrity and videos of cats. The complicated issues, the issues that matter to him, they take too much focus away from sexting, Snapchat, binge-watching the next hot vampire series. The truth?

The truth is hard to watch, hard to speak, hard to listen to.
All that distracts is so attractive.

Within each person there is a world reaching others, creating reactions, making connections. We have a voice. You are a world. I am you and you are me. But if a voice is not used, a truth not spoken or heard, then a whole world is lost. We all are the no man in no man's land. Lost, tired, crazy. It almost seems not worth it. Almost.

Me, I'm in it for the stillness of summer, the warmth of sand, sun on his skin, the drop of sweat that rolls and pools on his stomach. I bring the heat, turn all the levels to 11, sneak tiny shocks of static down to my fingertips. I want to catch him when he falls and show him how to burn. I'm in it for the fire.

I'm in it for the heartbeats, the legs stretched, in veins, scars and smiling teeth. I'm in the one step closer, the dance, the skin to skin, hand to hand, head on a shoulder. I'm in the breathing in the scent of another. I'm in it for the whispers, the subtext, the blank page, the smell of a new notebook, in the poems written till hands cramp and words hit the floor.

I'm the bend of his knees. I'm the taste of his lips. I'm the mess of his bed. I'm the Poetry.

*One boy. One girl. And love as simple as the sun.*

*Imagine the getting to know each other. Imagine the thousand Facebook messages, texts, emails, letters and scribbled notes on fridge doors.*

*Imagine two puzzle pieces clicking in – effortless. Imagine connection. Imagine togetherness.*

*But I didn't have to imagine. I was here.*

*I was here listening to their dawn conversations and the sound of heads leaning on shoulders.*

*I was here watching their hands find each other.*

*I was here for all the moments that flicker and sparkle in memory.*

*And I was here when she told him it's not love.*

# CALLING IT

You have a friend.

# THE SPARK

From the first time you meet and every time after you notice this
little spark. The something that whispers inside. The you and
me that could be we. The *I know you* and *tell me everything*
between our eyes. So you start to dance.

You know the dance. The dance like flirting but platonic –
you do coffee, you hang out, you message your favourite poems,
you have dates – not date dates, but times when time flies
and hours slow – peeling off your secrets like clothes
on the way to the bedroom, and you laugh and you talk
and you argue and you forgive and you love

and the spark is growing with the smiles that speak
of the better me when I'm with you and the better you
that you show me. Friends. It's just friends.

One evening you're both more than a little drunk,
banter and teasing turn into looks a fraction too long,
the distance between your bodies shrinks to millimetres.
It's late.
You snuggle in bed.
Sleep is tugging at your toes but skin is touching skin.
Hands wander stroking where clothes are not.

You don't talk.
You don't kiss.
You don't look, but your bodies push and pull closer and closer,
and it feels
so fine.
When you do kiss, it's tender and easy and loving.
You're naked.

Call it attraction.
Call it drunkenness.
Call it the spark.
Call it right.

Call it wrong.

# BREATHE

Your friend holds you tight and says, *I want to, oh, I want to.*

It's late.

You are in bed, naked and no longer drunk.
The thoughts of after and in the morning
waking up write themselves large.

You imagine a crystal glass friendship

that you don't want to smash with a fling
of drunken arms and artful moves.
And you talk and you argue and you laugh
and you forgive and you love.

Call it attraction. Drunkenness and the spark.
Call it right. Call it wrong. Call it anything you like.

I call it friends.

*He didn't come to visit me for weeks after that.*

*I stood forgotten, learned to count time.*

*I remembered the stories he told me about his mother who liked to drink coffee and his father who liked to hit her. How he learned to stoke and bank his rage and write it all in the night.*

*How he gave his sister to her demons.*

*How he became a boy who talks to trees.*

# CROSSED ROAD

It was an ordinary day, the day you told me
we were leaving home. Skipping my way
to school, I was cat-curious and sun-happy.
You wore Silence on your face, reading

the distance to the gate for the precise
moment you would talk to me.
I chattered on, showing you
stones discarded on the path, pleased

by the deliberate countdown of your heels.
Before you sighed and prepared
your heart to shatter mine, I was playing
with the last ray of my sunshine.

You stopped, stilling my fidget,
stockinged knees on the cobbles,
sad smile levelled at my eyes.
You spoke of all the times I already knew.

The times when Daddy's voice would shake
the walls and rattlesnake the windows.
The times when fear came in first
and I hid outside pretending

it was a game. The times when one word,
one fork out of place landed us in a visit
to hospital. The times of pasta for breakfast
and empty bottles. You told me I was eight.

Past the age of reason and excuses
enough to realise what my daddy is not.
Late for school, I carried the weight
of your words that circled and tied me down.

# A CUP OF COFFEE

Stone-cold, half-drunk, passed out on the kitchen
table in the morning run-rush, she ping-pongs
from sink to fridge to wardrobe, crash-tilt, throw
clothes on, shout, *Kids, where the fuck are your uniforms?*

Locate two (nearly white) shirts in the laundry
basket, knot ties, wipe faces and jumpers to hide
stains of odd socks, hunting again for one black shoe,
lunches packed, homework scribbled, out the door.

It's full-fat ground Columbian, drip-drip percolates,
milk-curdled thoughts dancing as she shakes like a wet
rag – the venom – hands cupped, hug in a mug of hate,
yummy mummies – the fishwives – glued to school gates,

judging, as they wag: the tattoos, bottle blonde, working
out the measure, tamped down, the up-down, she's drinking
one long swig, it's – vodka – numb to bruises,
words and hands smash-painted in black and blues.

A cup of coffee.

Hairline cracks in the day-to-day dishwater,
brown sugar holds the sides, tears like knives
scoring out graves to swallow the bitter espresso
blend to the finish last note.

# I KNEW MY PLACE

At the end of the table under the window, the long walk
to my chair, *don't run, take your shoes off when you come in*,
slippers polishing the hard wood and hard faces, *do
your homework*, the tick of the clock, *yes, you can play
if it's a quiet game, now wash your hands, time for dinner,
you don't have to like it, you just have to eat it.*
I knew my place.

They knew the empty plates, father and brothers not coming back.
They knew the last look at their home, wearing all their clothes
in layers, pockets stuffed with food. They knew not to say
goodbye to their school friends, the leaving at dawn, *walk,
don't run*, the slow race out of town.

They knew no time to grieve, not to see the body of the bakery
girl. They knew selling principles when you can't eat money
*but half a loaf is better than none.*

I knew my place. Eat up what's on my plate. They knew the war.

# HOMEGROWN

The day is for school and homework and waiting.
Waiting for my daddy to come home, alert
to the slap of his feet and the door hinges,
to the metal of his tools striking the floor, making me jump.
On the whole, I preferred the shouts to the Silence.
I could tell where he was in the flat from the rumble.

I started to write because I was afraid. I started
because no one would know. My secret.
It could not be taken away. I started when I realised
even my clothes smelled of alcohol and of that ground-in sweat
that lingers when someone has been drinking so long the smell
has stuck to every other surface.

I would only write at night. Climbing from my bed,
stepping over the snoring crocodiles, slow step by slow step.
Going to the bathroom is allowed at night. If you're quiet.
I open the fridge and write by the light,
the small white pages like a path to a world of colours.
I write the green of forest, the blue of open skies,
the red of wild strawberries in the grass.

And the iron tang of blood.

# LIKE A TON OF LEGO BRICKS

I carried my bed of roses home where
they teach the children not to be,
how to kill chickens before they hatch,
how the slap of a hand is more cutting
than the sharp of a word.

Mother was busy cooking curtains
into arguments, stirring the pot of radiator music.
Father's chair smelled of damp dinners,
he on his knees, picking up the crumbs
of you'll be a man, my son.

I came in, hid all the locks, shook out the mildew,
laughed myself out of my shackles and flew.

*Spring was close when he came back.*

*He sat with his arms round my trunk and with words crammed in like hummingbirds on his tongue, he told me: Sakura, I don't know any more. She comes and she goes like a dance of sunsets whispering I got it wrong. She gave me this letter.*

# NEVER GENTLE

The first time we had sex it hurt.

You were scrawled all over my body – nail to knuckle – outlined in
the bites on my neck, the tremble of my thighs. You clawed me open
up against a wall and kissed my lips bloody. It was rampant
and I loved it.
*We were never gentle, were we?*
We were clothes still on and mouth on mouth and *oh my god*
I need to have you right now. We were on the kitchen counter.
In the corridor. Up the stairs. On the bed, off the bed, on the floor.
It was picking you up from work at 2am and shagging

till the music of seagulls and bin lorries had faded and it was
drinking rum and carpet burns and feeling your heart beat
and telling each other our secret stories and listening
to your poetry, keep going, arms stretched back and *fuck me.*

But oh, how heat does burn.

And it was late nights *we need to talk* and *don't you fall in love
with me* and *it's just a thing* and *we must have some boundaries*
and *where is this going* and I and you and we are both in love with
someone else and *you bitch* and *fuck you.*

We were never gentle.

We were the storm and we were wild and we were naked.
Naked bodies and naked souls and naked hearts and never gentle.
It was fire, sweat dripping under your belly and eyes to eyes
saying *yes harder* and *do you want more.* It was your smile
like lightning and your hands scoring my skin and *don't stop.*
And it was finding you in my bed asleep one morning
and it was the very first time I wanted to say *I love you* but didn't.
It was hungry and devastating and we agreed *let's not go there.*

And all those nights and days and weeks and all the words
we spoke to each other. Sometimes I want gentle.
But not with you.

Passion ravageuse ...

# SMILE

Age five. When you're told to kiss Granny but she's got
these teeth and smells funky – *Smile, sweetie.*
When it's the school photo, look pretty, say cheese and smile
when the only choice for clothes is pink frilly on the girl side
of the shops and no one will pass the ball to you
in the playground but you just smile in frustration at yet another
party invite in gender-based colours, the segregation of toys,
games and stationery. So you smile, giving a card
on Mother's Day to your mum who is far too busy cooking,
cleaning, don't forget the laundry, to thank you.

You keep your smile. When at work, you're being explained
your own man-recycled ideas and start every sentence with
*I'm sorry, I would like to suggest that*— if you smile when in the
bus, train or at a gig you feel this hardness rubbing against your
leg and you pretend not to notice with a big wide smile
when you're getting a drink at the bar and *no I have a boyfriend*
does not register as a correct answer when a hand creeps
up your skirt and you want to scream but you smile
because it's safer to be called a *tease* and *slut* than to feel

fingers on your throat squeezing the smile when sleeping
and your partner sticks it in and you lie there wondering
*is this rape* and you go to the bathroom to clean up the mess
between your thighs and you smile when your friend asks
*what is this* when she sees your face and you tell her *it's fine*
or *I walked into a door* or *I fell down the stairs – I'm so clumsy* –
and you know that she knows but you both smile
when you walk home to the sound of footsteps and you grab
your keys till they bleed and you smile.

# SWEET FANNY ADAMS

Step. Breathe. Step. Breathe. Step. Breathe.
Stop. Look behind. Stop.
You lowered my eyes. Stop.

Where are you running to, girl?

See the scorn in the shoulders.
The hand that was raised.
The scorn, the hand, the teeth, the spittle, the—

You gotta go somewhere when you run, no?

Run. Yes. I run. From and because and over and under and from
and away. I run. Somewhere, anywhere, elsewhere, away. I run.
From the whites of the eyes and the chains of cruel to be cruel.
I run, because can you see the speed of Darkness in its black
jersey and the full of night is not far behind on the inside lane—

Why are you running? Again. You know there is nowhere to go.

I run from under the edge of a star, slide and skid on its corners,
grind away its sparkle with the stamp of my feet. I run over
the distance, the scheming melodies, the rise of the unspoken
no from my gut that never quite reaches my swollen throat.
I run to feel, the wind on my face erasing the mark of the hand
that was raised, again and again.

Sit down, girl. Looks like you could do with a swig of this. Thirsty
work, running.

I run for, for the oh-so-fragile glow of a small candle wavering,
wavering in the crush of air the hand that is raised forges,
again and again, the scorn in the shoulders, the teeth biting
stone-shaped words, the spittle burning when it lands on my
cheek, the blood… the blood inside the palms of my hands
when
I press my nails to the knuckles to stop the—

Do you even know what sound hopeless makes?
Have you smelled a belly-down grovel?
Can you taste the never again?

Girl, I taste it. I smell it. I hear it. This bottle, see, that's my run.
I drink down the happy, I swallow hard the embers of the dreams
that are stuck behind my eyes. This bottle, girl, with it I notice
the colour of a single word, I replay the terrible gestures unsaid
sentences compose when no one is paying attention to them.

Let me have a drink, I'm thirsty.

Now can you smell the forgiveness? Like the crackling ozone
of sudden summer rain that comes in, a thief picking
your pockets. Or is it more like fresh-cut grass mingled
with the half-remembered scent of the bread Mother
used to bake on Sunday mornings?

No. It is the smell of a baby-girl head before her first ever turn
in the bath, her face framed by the tears Mother shed
when she gave her a first and last kiss on the day she left me
here. It is the smell I decided to forget the day I finally ran and
turned into the boy who does not smile.

*One boy. One girl. The boy loved her with a love as simple as the sun.*

*I drank both in and felt green growth starting to sprout from my branches. Spring had returned.*

*The boy was down by my roots, writing and writing and writing till the crumpled paper by his side looked like winter. He sat and stared at blank pages and when night came in he fell asleep with a frown, hands full of the words he couldn't write down.*

*In the morning, he sat on the bench of trouble.*

# ON BEING TOLD TO SNAP OUT OF IT

You spit in the wind of change. You try your luck: still green.
Cash cows just aching to be fake-liked and twittered.
The germs of your insanity float and sprout dandelions
so damn tough to weed out. I will love you in the morning
any time when you command: *Keep your hands between your legs.*

You spit in the wind of change. You chuckle, *Oi oi saveloy
and a bottle of rum.* You try your luck: still green.
The tube is not responsible for delivering delays. It's the drivers.
Same everywhere. Are you looking carefully?
The magic will start right about now.

You spit in the wind of change. Where are the clouds gone?
I can touch the sky. You try your luck: *oh-oh.*
*This is not the place. This is not the time. This is not the same.*
Yesterday I was asleep when the postcard came.
The words got me up and told me everything I never needed to know

You spit in the wind of change. You don't play the game
or the piano and now you won't marry butter.
You try your luck and find the door wide open.
Your name is not she/her unless written under the stamp.

He/she tries spitting in the wind of change.
I was saving my luck for times like these.

# SITTING ON THE BENCH OF TROUBLE

shoes check trousers check coat check
five fingers five toes check check

I sit quietly so the wind won't see me.
I sit carefully so trouble won't find out.
I sit on my knees so the alligators can't get to my five toes.

beanie hat check nose check scarf check
five fingers five toes check check

The wind catches my sleeve but I tell him to let go.
The wind tries for my scarf; ha ha, I've tucked it in.
He gives up. He gives down sometimes, but I am never there.

shoes check trousers check coat check
five fingers five toes check check

Trouble starts to squirm behind the bushes.
He whistles close. That's my bench, you know.
I do. I know. But five fingers five toes I must sit.

shoelaces check trousers check coat check
five fingers five toes check check

# BLANK PAGE

There's something about a blank page.
The words you write, they trick your heart not to engage.
It's like dipping your pen in shadow, like believing
you're writing Tomorrow.

It's like trying to alphabetise your rage. It's like Jacob wrestling
angels. Write. Rewrite. Edit. Craft, then forge. Polish, polish,
polish. The ebb and flow. The new stuff needs time to grow.

There's something about a blank page.
Everything is pretend, even pretending to pretend.

Nothing touches you. You are uncaring. You don't like or dislike
but prefer to contemplate. You're doing your best impression
of Nero, back to the blackboard, lift muzak playing
whilst everything around you burns.
And yes, this last year has been wild. Some good wild,

some bad wild, but all through it, the fucking was wild.
You remember the wild far too vividly.
Can't you remember the glorious spots of clarity?
You do remember the stepping out of reality.
That's the stillness that sits between us, the quiet revelation
that light does have shadows.

There's something about a blank page.

You wrote the three words. I get it. The way our friendship
panned out. The crossing through minefields with blindfolds.
At the end of the woods, always more woods, no single step
or dance move to bend to the pitch of your emotion.

You bounce hard, all through the angles in a no-one-left-to-
fight-but-yourself kinda way.

# YOU HIDE, YOU COUNT

They drive you moonfaced moonstruck moon-blind to Bedlam
Court, Fear Castle. All the way through the antiseptic corridors
I drag you by the hand. A copycat Nurse Ratched hustle-bustles
you inside the secure ward, slamming the doors on my goodbye.

The words I wanted to say tiptoe away.

You hide, uptight in your Silence, blanketed
in your unsaid. Inside your mind, you walk
and talk and walk, jumping over pools
of language, playing hopscotch with echoes.

You sit on the wooden floor, thoughts like tiny
diamonds you stroke until they purr. You hide.

I count the hours, midnight and all is not well.
I bang my drum, make strawberry and heartbreak jam.

I count the days, nearly autumn. I hang
salmons and my salty tears out in the smoking shed.

I count the years and wait.
I don't go looking for your hiding place.

I shout: *Ollie, Ollie, in you come, free.*

# LEARNING TO SING THE BLUES

I woke up this morning
to red sun and shadows
stretching out. I slinked
fast past drilling tongues,
tap-tap-tap-wag-wag-wag.

I woke up this morning
to slice thick wedges
of butter, smirked, age-burnt
toast falls, slick-slick-slick
on the marmalade floor.

I said *you're it* and *no it back*.
You didn't padlock cross keys,
you stared and stared. I sat
holding your cold hand till
sirens came to drown you home.

*He cried that morning.*

*I wished I wasn't a tree then, to hold him and give him the words that comfort. To say that love doesn't always burn like the sun.*

*I didn't. I couldn't. I listened.*

*He raged for a long time, and when the Silence came I knew this was his last visit. He walked down the hill. I listened until summer, tended to my crown of blossoms and hoped.*

*And one night when the air was so clear it shone, the girl walked up the hill and she talked to me. All through the night she talked. She told me the stories that can only be spoken when the stars are bright,*
*because they cut to bone.*

*What had happened to her one Saturday night many years before. How she covered herself in filth so that her outsides matched her insides.*
*How she was left in the tallest tower of the darkest castle.*
*How the boy was a dream and she could only wear midnight.*

*I listened.*

Les affres de l'amour
((ego et cie!)
ego quand tu nous tiens ...

# LAST NIGHT

I was wearing the same clothes you see me in right now.
Except not torn, not bloody, not ripped, not muddy.

Now, I'm wearing
black around the eyes,
cuts on my forehead.
I'm wearing bruises on my inner thighs,
bite marks on my breasts.

It's the non-stop-flashback-catcalling-footsteps-whistling-wolf-
pack-nipple-twisting-hands-full-of-fingers.

Am I telling the truth?
I wasn't drunk. Not very drunk.

He roots and snuffs through my body
pressing down the weight of ten pints. I'm straining
neck muscles as far as my back can tight-fit against wet concrete.
His lips must not, must not, must not—
He grabs my throat with a whisper.

Do you feel me?

# SNAFU

I keep my eyes shut to stop revving full throttle, dreaming of cotton wool and the land where little girls in pigtails still believed. I could not fail to hear the chittering of my hair growing and the exquisite crinkle of aluminium. You looked up, soot on your face, and booted up the last dregs for all you were worth, which was much less than a grain of sand in the Sahara. Out of bed, out the flat, out to lunch. I did not say a word. I didn't look back. I didn't swear. I hit the streets full tilt and an extra ball in play, squeezing the throats of scurrying hopes and scaring babies in prams. My cluck and I, careening down the slim serrated edge of the pavement, climbing the walls that are – not – there. I swallow down the chunks of three-days-ago munchies that fill my mouth. Shivers catch up with me, biting hard and shaking me inside out. I subdue the spasms, give the starved-dog look a punch in the face and scan the horizon for the smoke signals of the something-something. My hands twitching as I peel my eyes off, pillaging my brain for who's got. Very soon, before I dissolve, I would say anything, I would sell anything, I would steal anything.

# IF YOU TELL

This is between us, sweetie. Our little secret. You and me.
Come a bit closer. Now, what are these tears for?
Don't play coy. Sit on my knees. Or I will burn your teddies.
That feels good. Yes. Unzip me. You should be ashamed.

Good little girls don't dress like you do. Of course I love you.
I wouldn't do – this – if I didn't love you. If you say no
I promise I will stop right now. Nothing to say?
You are the only one who understands me. Open wider.

This hurts me more than it hurts you, sweetie.
Now look what you made me do. Stop this crying.
If you don't like it, you only have to say stop.
Go clean yourself up, pull down your top and listen

very very carefully. This never happened.
No one will believe you if you tell because
you're such a naughty child. If you tell
the police will take me away and it will be your fault.

You and your brother will be put into care.
If you tell, everyone will know you liked it.
They will call you a dirty skanky lying bitch if you tell.
I will start again with your little brother.

This is between us, sweetie. Our secret. For you and me.

# FORTY-EIGHT

Little slivers of hate curled up in the morning.
7am, the hour for an early shriek. Closed curtains,
nothing to see here. I moved to London.
And still I expected the knives to come back.
I go round and round and left and right and up
and down sometimes. I hold my new keys my new
nose my new job close. I keep my head down but
I don't drown.

Little slivers of hate curled up at midday.
The sunlight steps over my shoulders – silent kitchen bruises.
My face pressed to the lino, I notice the speck of dirt you wanted
me to see. I make a list of all the constellations, under my breath,
to tune out the stench of your blows.

You pull my skirt up…
You tell me you are doing this because you love me, too much.
I say nothing. I wait.
Even after the sulphur of your grope has dissolved,
I wait.

Little slivers of hate curled up in the evening.
The moonlight fringes my gloved fingers – red-eye flight.
In the hush space before the slam-bang of the front door
I pause
and look at the racked knives.
Smooth soft slender blades
slash slit stunned furrows in your neck.

I had counted to forty-eight when you stopped moving.

*The heat starts early in summer.*

*I want to look at a spider crossing through the moon, a long drag
on a cigarette, mouths filled with sighs and two hands close but not
touching. I want to count on fingers made of salt, sunsets of flashing
green, waves flowing to sand and numbers that fail to add up
to the sum of their want.*

*But I am alone. Rooted to my hill. No sparrows, no foxes, no hedgehogs.
Her body weighs from the scarf on my tallest branch.*

*The heat starts early in summer.*

*My name is Sakura. I'm the tree who listened.*

# IT SHOULDN'T BE CALLED LIFE

The 5am rise and shine.
The daily grind, coffee with extra shot.
And what is the name you are writing on my cup?
It's overworked, underpaid, too many qualifications
and no fucking job satisfaction. Don't forget email apologies
must not start with the word *unfortunately*.
Unfortunately, we're giving you a zero-hours contract.
No, these are not alternative facts.

I see the way you look at me, like I'm a grenade
and you're waiting for me to go off. I make no excuses.
I am what I am. I burn like electricity.

But I don't fight it anymore; I only watch the bees.
I know you want something, answers. The thing is,
I'm having a difficult time figuring out what's real.
Life feels like I'm always on the other side of the bar, a captive
shrink with unlimited supplies of alcohol, looking at everything
from the bottom of the empty glass metaphor.

It's the questions that drive us, the hows and whys and therefore.
Because we live in a sorry universe engineered to create
this conflict. And we're all so sorry. I'm sorry that you bumped
into me. I'm sorry for your inconvenience except not really.
I'm sorry your dog died, or was it your baby?

I'm sorry to tell you that I'm sorry, sorry, sorry.

People, nice people, like me and you, they want to believe
there's more to it than this. Because if you believe
then you're innocent. But for the guilt that comes
out of your pores, a stink you fight to ignore as you breathe
it in and out. So you go out, meet other nice people.
The real you? Well, it's all tucked in, under the make-up,
the smart clothes you wear, under the smiling, all that pretend
confidence (it's all lies).
If they knew the real you.
The nasty thoughts you tend to edit out.
The way that you feel when you lie.
Cheat.
Have sex with your friend's one and only.
Imagine that on a giant screen.
Or don't.
Look it up on Facebook.

# IT SHOULD BE CALLED HYPOCRISY

We're all the same. We all have secrets, problems, regrets.

So here is my advice you didn't ask for.
Decide to be fine till the end of the week.
Make yourself smile because you're alive.
Do it again the next week and do it right, with a smile.
Live your life every day because it's your job.
Even when it hurts so much you'd rather pull
out your fingernails with pliers while listening to the radio.

Say things like *It's all my fault.*
*The good, the bad, I'm responsible.*

So what's the plan exactly?
Don't fucking die. Live.
Don't let fear get in the way, waiting for that moment to strike.
When you're weak. When you're sad. When it rains.
Live. Love. Grow some dreads.

Maybe it's all simpler than you think.
You find a cause and you serve it.
A reason to get up in the morning.
The savage thoughts. The guilt. The hurt.
They tend to shift over time.
We learn. We grow.
We find what makes our heart skip.
Life is beautiful.

But nothing in our lives is ever that simple.

SAKURA: fleurs de Cerisiers

petit pinceau
japonais sur
feutre humide

pinceau japonais
et parallel pen | branches

Pentel

petit pinceau
japonais

parallel pen

trancolo
P. b.B

Attention
papier
poreux
faire essai
sur
papier
tissu

# IT GOES WITHOUT SAYING

You have a way of keeping honest that terrifies me.

It's the sideways in your look, the crinkle in your frown.
I have no words. You turn your eyes, hands plus heart
wide open. A silent offer. I retreat in my unspoken, chat to you
about the weather. You chuckle. I keep on Oscar Wildeing.

You don't ask the questions pushing through the lines
of your face, like daffodils in spring. You make tea. You don't say
what's up with that coat of many hurts, that scarf of 2am staring
at the cracks that I've got hanging off my back. You give me
the quiet – moments of following the wind, playing with trees,
naming each strand of a spider web.

\*\*\*

I hold tea in the tremble of my hand and breathe in

your tenderness. The icebergs in my belly start to melt, teardrop
by teardrop, salting my cup. I don't drink. You don't say
everything will be okay, this too shall pass and tomorrow
is another day. Instead you explain in detail how your black
madam of a cat dropped a frog in your lap at breakfast time.
A not-quite-dead frog you cradled back into life.

That frog was good at pretending, you say.

Yeah, like me. I'm so good at that, I get cramps in my cheeks
from the fakeness of my teeth.

Until you reach in
with your sun-filled hugs, pluck broken tiles from my heart
and, with care, place each sharp edge next to another in a mosaic
that spells love. I want to shout *STOP*.

It's the thing of things. The feeling of feelings. If I had to put
my finger on it, I would trace it back to all we've not articulated
but doodled on the margins, words I shattered like a vase.
I'm barefoot, and it's death by a thousand small cuts.

Until you reach in
with the wide brim of your grin, you tell me: it's the centre
that holds us back, love has no gravity, there'll be days that
make sense, days that will bounce and days white-knuckling it.
You say we will be dancing in each other's jumpers that fit so
seamlessly.

But I can't.

# KOBAYASHI MARU

Write a little about yourself. Write a little. Write.

Write your story, add colour, no fiction, put feelings in their
place, not too many hundred-dollar words or adjectives and think
of where to stick the commas, like here should be good,
but you reread and it seems that maybe
some other punctuation could work.

I write the words that are not said when gestures cannot be read.
I write the intimacy of the near touch when you look long
and hard at the horizon and you can see tomorrow. Or the beach.
Or tears rolling down a face. Or stars. Or nothing. Or this.

Some Sundays you wake up when the birds are singing
and the sun is shining that sharp bright light that cuts
through the corners of your eyes to the ones in your mind
and you think good things, good things could start here,
that if you blink through the tears, it's like the song says
it's a brand new day and I'm feeling. I'm feeling.

It wasn't always like this.

I was born straight out of Dickens, a bad penny, passed
from hands to hands further away, sent like a postcard
to distant relatives that says *it's raining – wish you were here.*
Early on, I learned that rage could be a currency, hate
could protect me. So I decided to become ruthless, in order to
survive. If that means killing the part of myself that makes
being alive worthwhile… *Kobayashi Maru.*

That's when I found the beat.

It starts in your hair. Sweat-damp sticking to your eyelids,
you move. Head neck shoulders hips legs feet to arms hands
fingers vibrating. The beat. It feels like waiting to be struck
by lightning but there's nothing but blue in the sky.

Some Sundays when you've danced all night, you wake up
and the blue of the sky is so sharp that all the colours spill out
from your skin and from the edges of your eyes to the ones
of your mind, you think good things.
Good things could start here.

# THE NOTE

The sky is blue. The sky should be blue.
There are no clouds today. It's your birthday.
We play Simon Says.
Simon says hop on one foot. I hop. Sam hops. It's his birthday.
A boy from today and the sky is blue. I hop.

Coins in my pocket make a pleasant sound.
Enough coins for the meter today. I smile.
The sky is blue. It's Sam's birthday.
He chose the girl in the music shop.

Simon says no. Not enough coins for a girl and the kettle.
The sky is blue. There are no clouds today.
You have electricity and a kettle and Simon says
smile, Sam, it's your birthday.

# TIGER TIGER

This I remembered.
I chose to ride the tiger.
Told myself: this is not a tiger.
This I chose. I knew it would hurt.

I counted the hours, the days, the weeks, the months
after the times when I could no longer picture your face.
I walked down streets to find myself lost in the desert.
The place where pain is. It's in my steps and the grit

in my teeth. It's in my hands and the way my arms fold.
It's in the letters unopened, the emails unread, the *no*
*I'm busy I can't make it tonight,* the staring the phone to silence
when it rings. Sometimes it's in the smiling too much
and laughing too much and drinking too much and fucking
too many people too much. Sometimes.

This I remember.
I choose to ride the tiger.
I tell myself this is not a tiger.
I tell myself I don't care if it hurts.

I choose to sit close from shoulder to arm to fingers
touching each other to hip, leg and feet moving
together. I choose talking for hours, watching
the stars till the sun rises pink, when one last fag
becomes ten or twenty. I choose
the long silent eye contact, the slow burn

and did you actually kiss me last night?
You smile-shrug yes.
Today I'm awake
with the feel of your lips.
We kiss. I learn your tiger ways.

Our laughter fell
from walls
like a thin child's fists.

# EPILOGUE

*It was a silence that had not been heard in the boy's house before that day. It started one morning as the kitchen clock stopped ticking. The silence grew from the lack of things that made noise to the way gestures are muted*

*when the awareness of a dead body in the next room*

*is remembered.*

*The small noises of breakfast-making and snatches of long-forgotten verse were gone.*

*The wind that shook walls, made the roof creak and shutters slam*

*all through last night departed by daybreak.*

*The boy realised that must have been the time the silence woke him.*

*He opens his mouth. To force screams or shouts, but the burn in his stomach like he's swallowed a hot coal will not let him speak out. He sits staring at the back of his hands, fingernails cutting little half-moons inside his palms. Hands are funny things.*

*There is a book open on the table. Two fingers of cold coffee in the blue chipped mug and his hand rests on the handle, no longer twitching or grabbing what is left of the day, no longer plucking at his eyelashes and laying them down one by one on the note.*

*It is hard to notice at first, but the silence seems bigger.*

1/2/3 + aquarelle.

① Reform

④/5 + feutre Rose

④ 11
ARTPen

⑦ feutre
SIGN

② Reform
sur
aquarelle
humide

⑤

⑧ feutre
pinceau
Japonai
(peti

⑥ le comptoir
des écritures

③ Tinhao

⑨ feutre
pinceau
(Kuratake

⑩

⑪ pinceau
Pentel
+ eau

Pentel + eau

⑫ Parallel Pen
et
pinceau ⚠ Attention
Japonai papier
transparent

→ ESSAIS de DIFFÉRENTS STYLOS PLUMES

# ACKNOWLEDGEMENTS

*Sakura* has lived in my head down to my bones for the last four years. I sit in my writing place, look back, and think, *How did I get here with a finished book?* It started many years ago, when I had so much to say but no words to express my insides, because life pressed in and down and left me voiceless. Writing *Sakura* was the last few steps climbing out of the pit and walking away.

I'm grateful to have a mother who inspired me to look up and look out, and taught me to never give up. She also painted the fabulous illustrations and cover for *Sakura*. Merci, Maman.

*Sakura* would not exist if I hadn't met a poet who was so full of poetry I started to write my own. He read my first poems, said carry on, took me to my first open mic, said do it, provoked me to improve, said pass it on, and sparked the Boy character by telling me that he spoke to a tree that listened. Thank you, my friend, for this and the epic clown ninja moves along the way.

To keep writing and finish any long-haul writing project, you need someone who is going to push push push, listen to your self-piteous whining and not be afraid to tell you where you're going wrong. I'm crazy grateful for my friend Matt who has been an ear and a shoulder, a rum-fuelled partner in fun times and a scorched-earth feedback giver.

I met a lot of wondrous people who galvanised me with their praise, feedback and constant encouragement. None better than my local poetry and fire-jam tribe who took me in and gave me heart. Special mention goes to Louise Keeley and Mark Berry for Freeway Poets and Lagan Legski for Verbal Remedies.

A poet does not work alone. We steal, glean and bask in the inspiration others provide, sometimes unknowingly. Here are a few who had a profound impact on my work with their own: Abe Gibson, Fay Roberts, Joelle Taylor, Helen Ivory, Jon Seagrave, Hannah Teasdale, Shaun Gary Palmer, Rachel Long, Toby Thompson, Raymond Antrobus, Zena Edwards.

I'm deeply grateful to the Burning Eye team for publishing my work, and many hugs are coming for Bridget, Clive and Harriet.

Sakura

A 97

Myriam San Marco is a poet, promoter and creative writing facilitator. As the Bournemouth Poet Laureate, Myriam San Marco has been leading a creative writing and development program for local writers with the support of Bournemouth Libraries.

She founded Word Makers and Silence Breakers in 2016: a collection of wandering wordsmiths, vagabond verbalisers and rhyming rebels working as workshop facilitators, bards, fools and muses at local festivals and one-off events. The Wordmakers host a bi-monthly spoken word showcase.

Abe Gibson described her performance as cutting to draw blood.

Her words have been published in *Boscombe Revolution, Interpreter's House, Poets' Republic, Message in a Bottle, Oddity, Curly Mind* and *I am not a silent poet.*

facebook.com/MyriamWordMaker

facebook.com/wordmakers

writeoutloud.net/profiles/myriamsanmarco